Cruising A

Abbreviated G

Cruise Ship Passengers

Alaska, USA

Skagway, Alaska, USA

Hubbard Glacier, Alaska, USA

Juneau, Alaska, USA

Icy Strait Point, Alaska, USA

Sitka, Alaska, USA

Endicott Arm & Dawes Glacier, Alaska, USA

Ketchikan, Alaska, USA

Dutch Harbor, Alaska, USA

Vancouver, British Colombia, Canada

Victoria, British Colombia, Canada

By: *Emile Baladi*

&

Susan Baladi

Acknowledgment: This quick tourist guidebook is the result of high condensation of the authors' extensive knowledge of Alaska's port of calls. This knowledge was obtained through many years of research and visits culminated with hundreds of lectures presented by the authors on cruise ships plowing Alaska's seas. Wikimedia and Google Earth Pro were two of other references utilized in the research and visual aids in this guide for which we are most appreciative and grateful.

Introduction: For over twelve years we conducted hundreds of lectures on cruise ships plowing all the five oceans of the world. At the end of each lecture, some of the passengers always asked us if they can purchase copies of the lecture. Most cruise ship passengers and other tourists are hungry for abbreviated information regarding the places they are going to visit. They will use the information to make their decision regarding what to see and which tour to take. The information should include what makes each tourist site important to visit. Cruise ships normally dock for only a few hours in each port. This publication integrates historical, geographical, meteorological and other applicable parameters regarding prioritized and recommended tourist sites of Alaska's port of calls. It makes each reader well informed to prioritize and select the most economical method to tour/visit these sites within the limited time that the ship will be in the port.

Table of Contents

Acknowledgement   3

Introduction   4

Alaska, USA   7

Skagway, Alaska, USA   16

Hubbard Glacier, Alaska, USA   25

Juneau, Alaska, USA   31

Icy Strait Point, Alaska, USA   41

Sitka, Alaska, USA   47

Endicott Arm & Dawes Glacier, Alaska, USA   54

Ketchikan, Alaska, USA   59

Dutch Harbor, Alaska, USA   68

Vancouver, British Colombia, Canada   75

Victoria, British Colombia, Canada   87

 **Alaska, USA**

Alaska: The largest state in the USA: Land area at **663,268 mi²** **(1,717,856 km²)**; over twice the size of Texas, the next largest state; larger than the combined area of the next three largest US states: Texas, California, and Montana; larger than the combined area of the 22 smallest US states; larger than all but 18 sovereign countries. Its southeast part welcomes hundreds of cruise ships annually.

The origin of the name: Alaska (Аляска) was named by Russian; derived from Aleut (object to which the action of the sea is directed); or derived from Alyeska (the great land).

Synopsis of History: About 20,000 years ago people crossed the Bering Land Bridge in western Alaska, during the last ice age. At the end of the ice age, they fan out throughout the rest of the continent. Eventually, Alaska became populated by several Native American groups:

> **Southeast Coastal:** The Tlingit, Haida & Tsimshian
> **Interior:** The Athabascans
> **The northern circumpolar region (the Eskimos):** The Iñupiat & Yup'ik
> **Aleutian Islands:** The Aleut

Russian Colonization: 17th cent. 1st Russian built settlement on Three Saints Bay on **Kodiak Island**, followed by several Russian vessels loaded with immigrants. By 1814 the Russian settlement of St. Paul's Harbor on **Kodiak Island** was established. The Russians colonized other parts. However, less than 1% of Alaska was ever colonized by Russia. This is because the colony was never profitable. However, Russia claimed all of Alaska.

Location of Kodiak Island

Russia Administration: Sitka became the capital of Russian America and remained the capital after the colony was transferred to the US. Evidence of Russian settlement in names & churches (examples: **Russian church in Juneau and Baranof & Chichagof Islands**, where **Sitka** and **Icy Strait Point** are respectively located).

Russian Orthodox Church in Juneau

Spain Connection: 1774-1800, several Spanish expeditions reached Alaska. By 1789 a Spanish settlement & fort were built which gave names to **Valdez, Cordova** (map below).

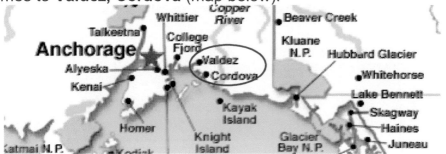

The Purchase: Oct 18, 1867, William H. Seward, the US Secretary of State, negotiated the **Alaska Purchase, $7.2 million** (~$130 million in 2019 USD), 2 cents per acre.

By 1877: **Sitka, located on Baranof Island** (see Sitka section in this book) was the only Alaskan community settled by American.

Copy of the $7.2 million Alaska Purchase Check

The Klondike Gold Rush: 1896-1899 The Klondike Gold Rush (will be detailed in this book under the Skagway section).

Modern History: 1906 the capital was moved from Sitka to Juneau. By 1912 Alaska was incorporated as an organized territory. Immigrants from Norway & Sweden settled in SE Alaska beefed up the fishing & logging industries.

WW II: Jun 1942-Aug 1943, 3 outer Aleutian Islands occupied by Japan (**Attu, Agattu & Kiska**). During June 1942, the Japanese Navy bombed Dutch Harbor (see map below). The U.S. Lend-Lease program flew US warplanes to Russia through Canada & Alaska.

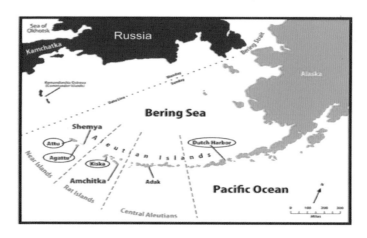

Alaska's Statehood: Jul 7, 1958, Congress approved statehood. Jan 7, 1959, Alaska became the 49th state of the United States.

Good Friday Earthquake: Mar 27, 1964, Magnitude 9.2 earthquake, history's 2nd-most-powerful earthquake. Resulted in the death of 133 people, the destruction of several villages and the creation of a major tsunami that destroyed portions of large coastal communities.

Anchorage after the Good Friday Earthquake

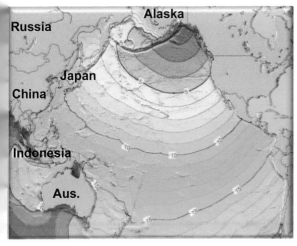

Travel Time Map for the Good Friday Tsunami

Red: 1- to 4-hour

Yellow: 5- to 6-hour

Green: 7- to 14-hour

Blue: 15- to 21-hour

Oil Discovery: 1968 vast amount of oil was discovered in the Arctic North Slope. By 1977 the 800 miles Trans-Alaska Pipeline System was completed which led to an oil boom that funded the state budget and repealed state income tax.

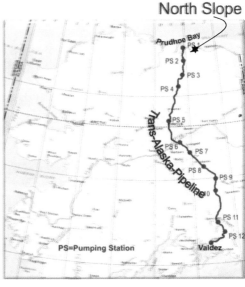

1989, the tanker Exxon Valdez: hit a reef in the **Prince William Sound** resulted in a major oil leak contaminating the pristine sound (see next map).

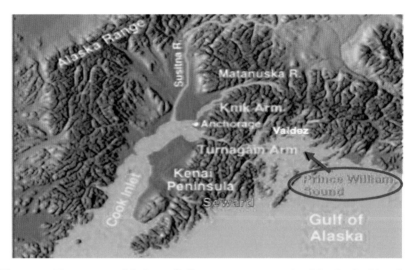

Alaska's Energy Reserve: Major oil & gas reserves in Alaska's North Slope (ANS) & other areas; Substantial coal deposits, 85.4 trillion ft^3 (2,420 km^3) natural gas; Vast potential hydroelectric power; Wind & geothermal energy potential.

Geography: North the Arctic Ocean; East Yukon & BC in Canada; South the Gulf of Alaska & the Pacific Ocean; West the Bering Sea, Bering Strait, Chukchi Sea & Russia.

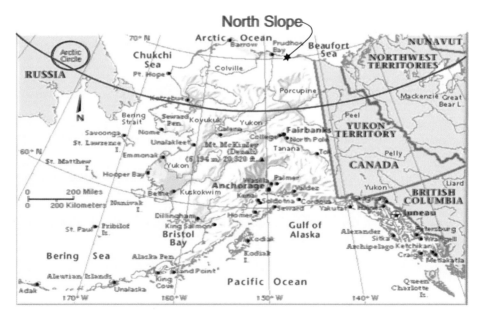

Unique Geography: US' Northernmost & westernmost state; Closest to the **Int'l Date Line***; The only non-contiguous U.S. state on continental N. America; Longer coastline than all the other U.S. states combined; Approximately 1/3rd of Alaska is west of Hawaii.

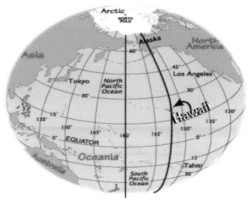

*International Date Line: Follows the meridian of 180° longitude, approximately in the middle of the Pacific Ocean; Turns to the east through the Bering Strait and then west past the Aleutian Islands. This way Alaska & Russia are on opposite sides of the line to keep the same date with the 2 respective countries.

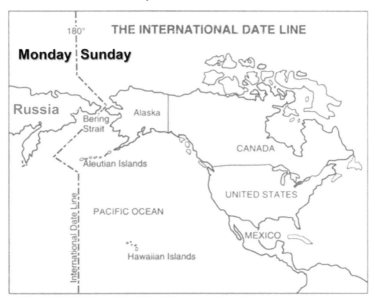

International Dateline

Economy: Oil & gas dominates the economy; seafood is second only to oil and gas.

Volcanism: Many active volcanoes most are in the Aleutians Islands (Part of the Pacific Ring of Fire).

Aleutian Islands Volcanoes

Alaska Marine Highway   Most cities and communities in southeast Alaska and east Aleutian Arc are located on islands and no road access connects these communities to the rest of the state and North America. Therefore, the Alaska Marine Highway was established. It consists of 3500 miles ferry service operated by the state and headquartered in Ketchikan.

Tides: Turnagain Arm, south of Anchorage, has one of the world's largest tides. It can reach up to 35 ft (10.7 m). Alaska has 1,200 mi^2 (3,110 km^2) of tidal zone, where at high tide, water covers the tidal zone land area.

Glaciers: Over 100,000 glaciers; ~1/2 of the world's; covers ~16,000 mi^2 (41,440 km^2).

State Symbols:

Motto: North to the Future.

Nicknames: The Last Frontier.

Bird: Willow Ptarmigan.

Fish: King Salmon.

Flower: Wild/Native Forget-Me-Not.

Land Mammal: Moose.

Mineral: Gold.

Sport: Dog Mushing.

Tree: Sitka Spruce.

 # Skagway, Alaska, USA

Location: Southeast Alaska, the ship sails through Lynn Canal to Tayia Inlet/Fjord. Skagway is at the end of this fjord. To reach Skagway, the cruise ship follows the yellow line on the Google Earth map next page.

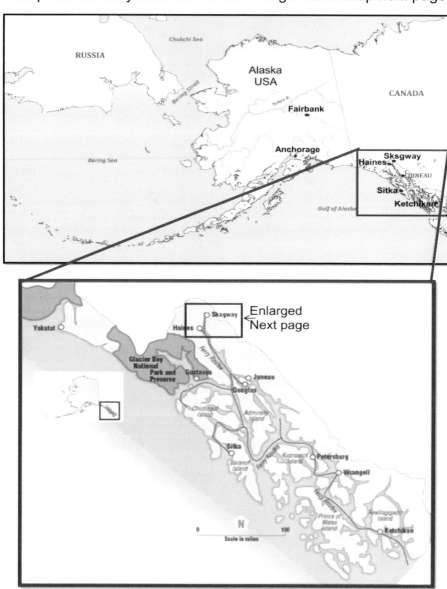

Location of Skagway

The Name Skagway: Derived from a Tlingit description of rough seas in the Taiya Inlet caused by strong north winds.

Synopsis of History: Inhabited by Tlingit (indigenous people) from prehistoric times.
In 1887, **William "Billy" Moore*,** discovered the White Pass over the Coast Mountains just north of Skagway. He believed that gold lay in the Canadian Klondike north of Skagway. Geologically, the Klondike is similar to mountain ranges in South America, Mexico, California & British Colombia where gold was found. Moore & his son claimed a 160-acre homestead at the mouth of the Skagway River. He believed it provided the most direct route to the potential goldfields. Moore and his son built a log cabin & facilities in anticipation of future gold prospectors passing through.

> ***Gold Discovery:** 1896, gold was found in the Klondike region near **Dawson****, the capital of Canada's Yukon Territory. Skagway was the closest land jumping point to the goldfields. 1000s of prospectors came to Skagway prepared for the 500-mile journey to Dawson*. The Moores were overrun by lot jumping miners & had their land stolen and sold to others.

**Dawson City, Capital of Yukon: The center of the Klondike Gold Rush. The population grew from 1st Nation (Indigenous People) camp to 40,000 by 1898. By 1899, the gold rush ended, the population plummeted to 8,000. 1953 Whitehorse replaced Dawson as the capital of Yukon (see map below).

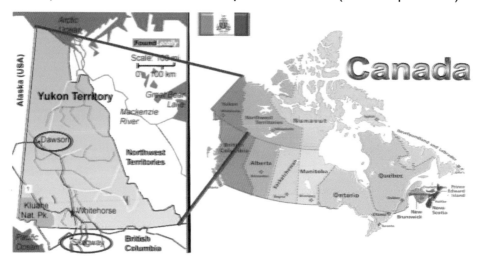

The Location of Skagway, Dawson, and Whitehorse

The Gold Rush of 1897-1898: Skagway was a lawless town. Fights, prostitutes & liquor were rampant. Con man **"Soapy" Smith*** raised to power. Canadian Northwest Mounted Police described Skagway **"little better than a hell on earth"**

*Jefferson Randolph "Soapy" Smith II (Nov 2, 1860 – Jul 8, 1898): He was a sophisticated swindler and generous benefactor to the needy. Operated a ring of thieves to swindle prospectors. On Jul 8. 1898 he was shot and killed and Interred at the Klondike Gold Rush Cemetery "Skagway's Boot Hill".

1898　　　　　　　　　　**2018**

Jeff. Smith's Parlor
Soapy's base of operations

Gold prospectors' journey: Climbed the mountains on over the White Pass to Bennett or neighboring lakes. Built barges & floated down the Yukon River to the goldfields around Dawson City. Others crossed northward on the **Chilkoot Pass/trail.**

Chilkoot Pass Trailhead

Preservations: To avoid starvation during the winter, Canadian officials began requiring that each prospector brings with him 680 kg supplies. Chilkoot trail stories are preserved in downtown Skagway at the Klondike Gold Rush National & International Historical Park.

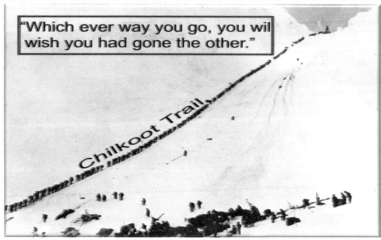

Chilkoot Trail

The Railroad: 1896, a group of investors saw an opportunity for a railroad over the gold rush route due to Skagway's deep-water port. 1898 construction began in Skagway.

The end of the gold rush: 1899 the stream of gold-seekers diminished. Skagway's economy began to collapse. By 1900 the railroad was completed, the gold rush was nearly over.

Road Connections: Skagway is connected to the Canadian road system via the Klondike Highway. This highway allows access to the lower 48 states via Alaska Highway through the Yukon and British Columbia.

The White Pass and Yukon Railroad: A Canadian and US Class II, 3 ft (914 mm) narrow gauge railroad links Skagway with Whitehorse, the capital of Yukon. It is an isolated system (has no connection to any other railroad).

Current Operation: In 1988 was revived as a heritage railway. Today operation is between Skagway & White Pass mostly for cruise ship passengers.

White Pass & Yukon Route Train

Skagway Population: ~1200

Tourism: Major part of the local economy. About 1 million visitors per year, 3/4ter of which arrive on cruise ships.

6-Major attractions:

1. **Klondike Gold Rush National Historical Park:** in downtown Skagway, walking distance from your ship.

2. **Chilkoot Trails*:** you need transportation, such as a rented car, to get to the trailhead, about 2 miles from downtown. (Follow the route marked yellow on the Skagway vicinity map below).

3. **The Historical District of the Gold Rush Era:** located in downtown Skagway (walking distance from ship).

4. **The White Pass & Yukon Route Narrow-Gauge Train Rides:** a short walk from the ship docks to the train. Train tours are normally booked early. For best sceneries, seat yourself on the left windows of the train going forward toward the mountains.

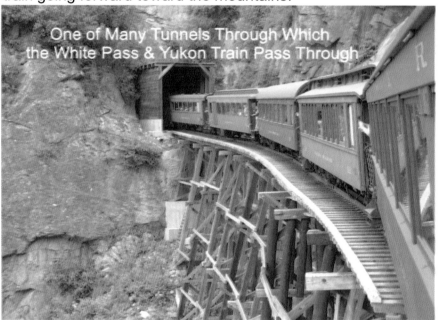

One of Many Tunnels Through Which the White Pass & Yukon Train Pass Through

5. **Hiking Various Trails:** trailheads are within walking distance from docks, trail maps are available from the ranger station in downtown Skagway.

6. **Carcross Desert:** if you've been to Skagway before and looking to do something else this time, one option is to rent a car (available in downtown) and drive through British Colombia to Yukon's Carcross Desert. The desert is located outside the town of Carcross, Yukon, approximately 65 miles from Skagway. It is considered the smallest desert in the world. Measures ~1 mi^2 (2.6 km^2) (640 acres). The highway to the desert crosses one of nature's most scenic and serene settings. You will pass by several sparkling lakes.

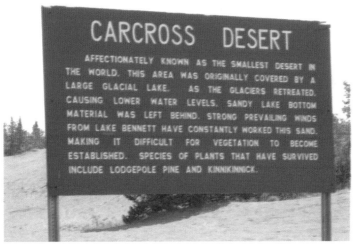

Cruise ship docks: Four large cruise ships berths are available for docking. Distance to downtown and major attraction is between 1/4ter of a mile and 3/4ter of a mile depending on the docking position. The location of the docks is indicated in the photo below.

Cruise Ship Docks

Climate data for Skagway, Alaska												
Month	**Jan**	**Feb**	**Mar**	**Apr**	**May**	**Jun**	**Jul**	**Aug**	**Sep**	**Oct**	**Nov**	**Dec**
Rec. high °F (°C)	52 (11)	60 (16)	59 (15)	76 (24)	82 (28)	89 (32)	92 (33)	91 (33)	77 (25)	68 (20)	59 (15)	52 (11)
Ave. high °F (°C)	27 (−3)	33 (1)	39 (4)	50 (10)	59 (15)	65 (18)	67 (19)	65 (18)	57 (14)	48 (9)	36 (2)	32 (0)
Ave. low °F (°C)	17 (−8)	22 (−5)	27 (−3)	33 (0)	40 (5)	47 (8)	50 (10)	49 (9)	44 (7)	37 (3)	27 (−3)	23 (−5)
Rec. low °F (°C)	−15 (−26)	−15 (−26)	−5 (−21)	14 (−10)	14 (−10)	23 (−5)	23 (−5)	23 (−5)	19 (−7)	8 (−13)	−6 (−21)	−14 (−26)
Ave. precip. In. (mm)	2.2 (55)	1.8 (47)	1.6 (39)	1.2 (31)	1.3 (33)	1.1 (28)	1.2 (30)	2.2 (56)	4.0 (103)	4.2 (108)	2.9 (73)	2.4 (62)
Ave. snow in. (cm)	14.2 (36)	9.7 (25)	3.3 (8)	1.0 (3)	0.1 (0)	0 (0)	0 (0)	0 (0)	0 (0)	1.2 (3)	8.6 (22)	11.1 (28)

Hubbard Glacier, Alaska, USA

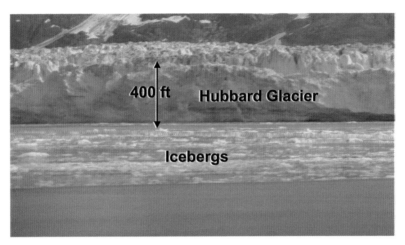

400 ft   Hubbard Glacier

Icebergs

Location: Located in southeastern Alaska & part of Yukon, Canada. To reach it from the sea, the ship Sails through the Gulf of Alaska to the 40 miles long Yakutat Bay to the 10 miles long **Disenchantment Bay***.

> ***Disenchantment Bay**: named by Spanish Captain Alessandro Malaspina, upon finding that the bay was not the entrance to the legendary Northwest Passage. He sailed up the bay before discovering the passage was blocked by ice. Therefore, he was disenchanted, thus, the name.

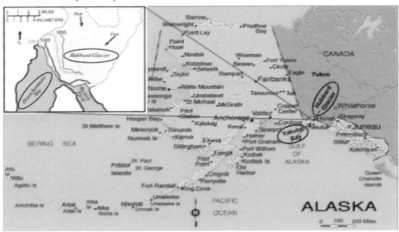

Glacier & Ice Field Formation: If successive snows do not melt completely in summer months, the snow would pile up year after year. The pressure of the weight of the snow would turn it into ice. If this ice is set on flat land, an ice field will form. On the other hand, if the ice is setting on an inclined land, such as a mountain's slope, then gravity will force the ice to slide down the slope and a glacier is formed.

The Name Hubbard: Named after Gardiner Greene Hubbard, Founder & 1st president of the National Geographic Society, Founder & the 1st president of the Bell Telephone Company (currently AT&T) and Founder of the journal *Science*. One of his daughters, Mabel Hubbard married Alexander Graham Bell.

Gardiner Hubbard

Hubbard Glacier: 122 km (76 mi) long from its 11,000 ft (3400 m) source in the Yukon. One of its tributaries begins on Mount Logan ridge ~18,300 feet (5,600 m), the highest mountain in Canada & the second-highest peak in North America. The ice at its foot is ~400 years old since its precipitation as snow.

Valerie Glacier: Joins Hubbard glacier's west side just before it reaches the sea.

Hubbard and Valerie are **Tidewater Glaciers*** and are currently surging. Their surges will eventually dam the **Russell Fjord** (map next page) from Disenchantment Bay. Russell Fjord will become "**Russell Lake**". This happened temporarily in 1986 & briefly in 2002.

> ***Tidewater Glacier:** a glacier that slowly, over many years, surges and retreats, as the ocean tide. Hubbard is the largest tidewater glacier in Alaska.

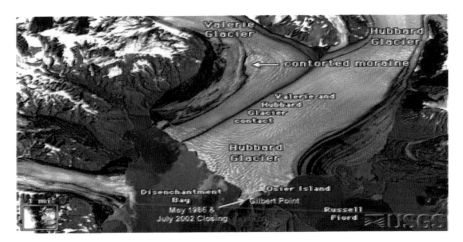

Russell Fjord to Russell Lake: May 1986, terminal **moraine*** closed the opening between Russell Fjord & Disenchantment Bay at Gilbert Point (maps above and below). May to Oct 1986 runoff raised the fjord water level to 25 m (82 ft) became Russell Lake resulted in salinity decrease which threatened its sea life. This happened again in July 2002. Both closing was temporary as the water pressure broke through these moraine dams and Russell Lake was back to Russell Fjord. It is expected to happen again, this time permanently, by 2030, and then Russell Lake could overflow its southern banks & drain through the Situk River, threatening trout habitat & a local airport (see map below).

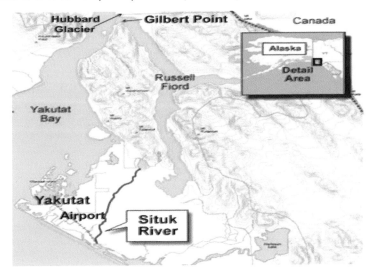

*Moraine: Any glacially formed accumulation of unconsolidated glacial debris. The debris is accumulations of rock, soil and sand scraped from the land as a consequence of glacier movements.
- Lateral moraines are formed at the side of a glacier.
- Terminal moraines are formed at the foot of a glacier.
- Medial moraines are formed where two glaciers meet.

The Ship Passage to Hubbard Glacier (see next map): From the Gulf of Alaska, the ship will enter the 40 miles long Yakutat Bay. The ship will sail for about 3 hours in Yakutat Bay before entering the 10 miles long Disenchantment Bay. The ship then will proceed at low speed toward Hubbard Glacier (about 2-3 hours). Various sizes of floating icebergs* will start to appear all over the bay. The Captain will sail the ship as close to the glacier as safely possible. The beautiful sceneries include glaciers and ice fields hugging incredibly high mountain chains. The best observation points on the ship are everywhere you can observe the magnificent sceneries. Therefore, observe the sceneries from every outside level of the ship and after taking a few photos and videos, put the camera/phone down and enjoy the magnificent nature with your own eyes.

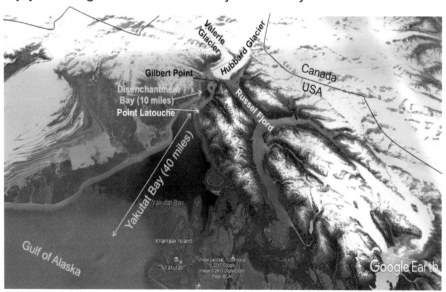

Map of the Entrance/Exit to Hubbard Glacier

*Iceberg Size Classifications		
Size Classifications	Height	Length
Growler	Less than 3' (1 m)	Less than 16' (5 m)
Bergy Bit	3'-13'(1-4 m)	15'-46'(5-14 m)
Small	14'-50'(5-15 m)	47'-200'(14-60 m)
Medium	51'-150'(16-45 m)	201'-400'(61-122 m)
Large	151'-240'(46-75 m)	401'-670'(123-213 m)
Very Large	over 240'(over 75 m)	Over 670' (over 213 m)

The Tip of the Iceberg: When water freezes, it expands and thus its density slightly drops below the density of surrounding water. That is why icebergs seem to float. Only 9% of an iceberg is above water, the rest of it, 91% is below the waterline.

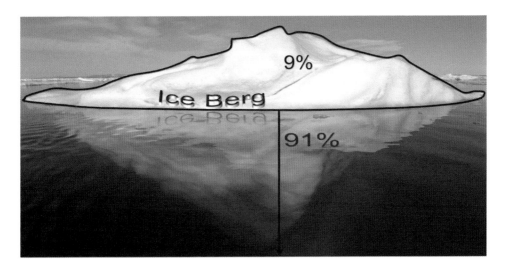

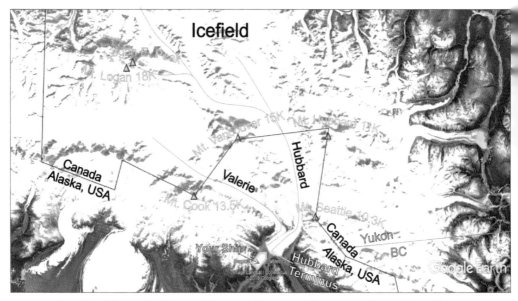

Ice Fields, Glaciers, Mountains and International Borders

 **Juneau, Alaska, USA**

Location: located in southeast Alaska on a narrow plane on a sea canal below two major mountains, mount Juneau and mount Roberts. Alaska's map below indicates Juneau's location relative to the state

The Name Juneau: named after gold prospector Joe Juneau. The Tlingit native name is Dzántik'i Héeni (means: Base of the Flounder's River).

Joe Juneau

Synopsis of History: Auke and Taku (indigenous tribes) fished the Gastineau Channel, where Juneau is located, for thousands of years before European settlement in the Americas. Their descendants include the current Tlingit people. Their cultures have rich artistic traditions expressed in carving, weaving, orating, singing, and dancing. Juneau has become a major social center for the Tlingit and other indigenous people of Southeast Alaska.

First European: 1794 The 1st European to see the area was Joseph Whidbey, part of **George Vancouver 1791-95 expedition***.

> *** The Vancouver Expedition** (1791–1795) was a 5 continents exploration commanded by George Vancouver of the British Royal Navy. The expedition included up to four vessels, 153 men, all but six of whom returned home safely.

Gold Discovery: 1880 gold nuggets discovered in the area. Soon a mining camp appeared. 1881 the camp became a small town, population 100 named Rockwell, Harrisburg then Juneau. Juneau was the first town after Alaska purchase on Oct 18, 1867.

Juneau in 1887

Capital to Juneau: By 1906 Sitka, Alaska's capital, declined in importance due to the decline of whaling and fur trade. The seat of government was then moved to Juneau. Juneau became Alaska's largest city until the end of World War II.

Locations of Sitka and Juneau

Area: US' 2nd largest city by area, larger than Rhode Island & Delaware. **Douglas Island** is part of Juneau. Two glaciers: **Mendenhall** and Lemon Creek are within the city limit.

US' Ten Largest Cities by Area

Rank	City	State	Land area (mi²)	Water area (mi²)	Total area (mi²)	Pop. (~K)
1	Sitka	Alaska	2,870.3	1,941.0	4,811.4	11
2	Juneau	Alaska	2,701.9	552.0	3,253.9	33
3	Wrangell	Alaska	2,541.5	920.6	3,462.1	3
4	Anchorage	Alaska	1,704.7	256.3	1,961.0	292
5	Jacksonville	Florida	747.0	138.0	885.0	822
6	Anaconda	Montana	736.5	4.7	741.2	8
7	Butte	Montana	716.2	0.6	716.8	34
8	Oklahoma City	Oklahoma	601.11	19.23	620.34	580
9	Houston	Texas	599.6	27.9	627.8	2,100
10	Phoenix	Arizona	516.7	1.2	517.9	1,446

Population: ~33,000, 2nd most populous city in Alaska, After Anchorage. Fairbanks is Alaska's 2nd most populous metro area (~100K).

De-Facto Island? Juneau has no roads connection to the rest of Alaska. No roads connection to the rest of North America. This is due to extreme rugged terrains surround the city. Only ferry & air services can reach the city. This makes Juneau a de-facto island city.

International geography: The only U.S. state capital located on an international border. Borders on the east by Canadian Province, British Colombia.

Transportation: State-owned ferries use the Alaska Marine Highway System (AMHS) (see AMHS in the Alaska section of this book). Local government operates a bus service, Capital Transit. Taxicabs, tour buses, and car rentals are available.

Trivia: Juneau is one of 4 state capitals not served by an Interstate highway. The other state capitals are: Dover, Delaware; Jefferson City, Missouri; and Pierre, South Dakota.

Juneau Access Project: Currently, fast car ferries to Haines & Skagway (~5 hours). The latest estimate for a road to Haines & Skagway is $590 million & rising with operation and maintenance cost ~$14+ million/year. Local opinion regarding the road project is mixed, about half for and half against.

Juneau Topography: Downtown sits just above sea level below steep mountains up to 4,000 feet (1,200 m) high. On top of these mountains is **Juneau Icefield**. **Douglas Island*** is a tidal island, set across Gastineau Channel. Douglas Island is part of Juneau.

> ***Douglas Island: A tidal island**** comprise of residential suburb within Juneau. Located to the west of Juneau and can be reached via the Douglas Bridge. The island is separated from downtown Juneau by Gastineau Channel.
>
>> ****Tidal Island:** when the tide is high, it is an island; when the tide is low it is not (see illustration next page).

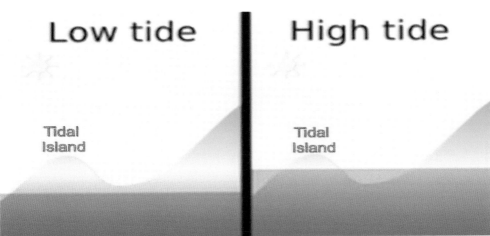

Illustration of a Tidal Island

Economy: The primary employers are: Government, tourism and fishing industries.

Cruise Ships Tourism: In 1990, about 230,000 passengers visited Juneau on cruise ships. By 2019 this number exceeded one million.

Major Attractions:

> **Whale Watching, Mendenhall Glacier, Helicopter Tours, Mount Roberts Tramway, Hiking, Father Brown cross, Red Dog Saloon, Patsy Ann and Kayaking:** you can take cruise ship tours or buy your tours from vendors located just outside the ship's dock security zone as shown below.

Private Tour Vendors Just Outside the Dock Areas

You can do some of the attractions by yourself for a fraction of the cost of joining organized tours. To do this your first stop should be at the Information booth located next to the Public Library just outside one of the cruise ship docks. There, you can collect information regarding the city bus schedule, routes, maps and direction to the attractions you want to visit.

Mendenhall Glacier: located at about 5 km from Juneau. The glacier is 22 km long, originates from the Coast Mountain Range at an elevation of about 1,600 meters. It has been receding for over 200 years. **you can go to Mendenhall Glacier for less than ten dollars by utilizing local bus and relatively short and easy walks.**

Mt. Roberts Tramway: Within walking distance from cruise ship docks. The tram ascends to 1800 ft of the 3819 ft Mount Roberts. The view from there is stunning. The cost is about $40 roundtrip. **However, if you hike (strenuous hike) the 1800 ft to Mount Roberts Tram stop (see trailhead map), you can ride the tram down free of charge if you spend $10 at the 1800 ft tram's restaurant and/or shops (keep the receipts).**

Mt. Roberts Tramway

Hiking: Some of the most beautiful hikes in Alaska are in Juneau. In addition to Mount Roberts, there are several trails into the mountains. The trailheads for most of these hikes are located on Basin Road. The most beautiful hike is the **Perseverance Trail** (see trail map).

Father Brown Cross: At 1800 ft Tram stop, a 2/3rd mile trail leads to a large cross named Father Brown cross. Father Brown was Born in Baltimore, MD 1860, attended Jesuit Loyola College (MD), Georgetown University (D.C.) & College of the Holy Cross (MA). Father Brown Initiated the construction of the trail.

View from Mt. Roberts Trail

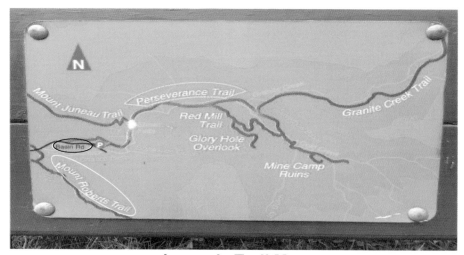

Juneau's Trail Map

Red Dog Saloon: Within walking distance from cruise ship docks. It is located on 278 South Franklin Street. The saloon has been in continuous operation since the mining era. The owners used to meet the tour boats at the docks with a mule with a sign saying, "Follow my ass to the Red Dog Saloon." The saloon hosted an episode of the Ed Sullivan Show after Alaska became a state. One of the mementos in the Saloon is **Wyatt Earp's pistol** as shown in this section.

Red Dog Saloon

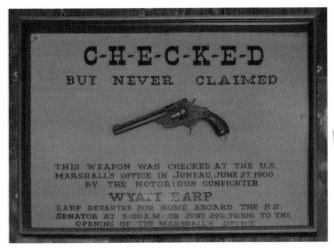

C-H-E-C-K-E-D
BUT NEVER CLAIMED

THIS WEAPON WAS CHECKED AT THE U.S.
MARSHALL'S OFFICE IN JUNEAU, JUNE 27, 1900
BY THE NOTORIOUS GUNFIGHTER
WYATT EARP
EARP DEPARTED FOR NOME ABOARD THE S.S.
SENATOR AT 5:00 A.M. ON JUNE 29th PRIOR TO THE
OPENING OF THE MARSHALL'S OFFICE

Wyatt Earp's pistol at the Red Dog Saloon

Patsy Ann: A Bull Terrier. Had an unerring sense of ship arrivals. Faithfully she welcomed each at wharfside. She died in Juneau in 1942 and was Buried in Gastineau Channel. A status of her is located on the boardwalk perched on pilings above Gastineau Channel welcoming cruise ships to Juneau.

Patsy Ann

Climate Data for Juneau

Month	Jan	Feb	Mar	Apr	May	Jun	Jul	Aug	Sep	Oct	Nov	Dec
Av. high °F	33	35	40	48	57	62	64	63	56	47	38	34
Av. low °F	24	25	28	33	41	47	50	49	44	38	29	26
Av. Precip. In.	5.4	4.1	3.8	3.0	3.4	3.2	4.6	5.8	8.6	8.6	6.0	5.8
Av. Snow. In.	28	17	12	1	0	0	0	0	0	1	13	16

Icy Strait Point (ISP), Alaska, USA

Location: Located on Chichagof Island, the **5^{th*} largest island in the US**, near the **village of Hoonah** (2miles away). Icy Strait Point is named after the nearby Icy Strait.

Location of Icy Strait Point

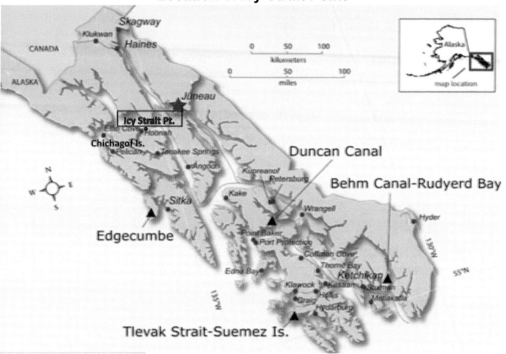

Rank	Island's Name	Area (mi²)	Area (km²)	Location	~Pop. K
1	Hawaii (Big Is.)	4,028	10,433	Hawaii	190
2	Kodiak	3,588	9,293	Alaska	15
3	Puerto Rico	3,363	8,710	Puerto Rico	4,000
4	Prince of Wales	2,577	6,675	Alaska	6500
5	**Chichagof**	**2,080**	**5,388**	**Alaska**	**1500**
6	St. Lawrence	1,983	5,135	Alaska	1500
7	Admiralty	1,684	4,362	Alaska	700
8	Nunivak	1,625	4,209	Alaska	200
9	Unimak	1,590	4,119	Alaska	40
10	Baranof	1,570	4,065	Alaska	9200
11	Long	1,401	3,629	New York	8,000

The 11 Largest Islands in the USA

Ownership: Icy Strait Point was developed and currently is owned by Huna Totem Corporation, Alaska's only privately-owned cruise destination. Most other destinations are owned by the cities in which they are located.

Synopsis of History: The Alaska Native Claims Settlement Act of 1971 stimulated the establishment of Huna Totem Corporation. After the corporation purchased the site in 1996, Icy Strait Point opened for cruise ships in 2004 using tender operation. In 2016 a 400 ft floating dock was installed allowing one large cruise ship to dock. The dock is connected to the information building of ISP with, mostly covered, **elevated walkway**. The starting point for all attractions is within a short distance from the information building. Currently, the cruise ship business accounts for about half of the local economy.

7-Major Attractions: Most tours are sold by the ship or local operator:

1. **Whale Watching:** ISP is probably the best location in Southeast Alaska to watch whales. The operators of the whale watch tours guarantee that they will find whales. Whale watching tours are operated by the corporation tour operators.

Whales at ISP can be anywhere

2. **Bear Watching:** About half an hour tour bus ride to areas where bears are expected. These tours are operated by the corporation tour operators.

3. **Zipline:** Consists of six side-by-side lines each is equipped with stopping spring. The zipping speed can reach 60 miles/hour. This

is one of the highest and longest ziplines in the world. Opened in May 2007; measures 5,330 feet (~1.01 mi) (~1.62 km) in length and 1,330 feet (410 m) drop from the mountain to almost sea level making it one of the highest in the world; rated a statewide "must do" attraction. The termination point of the zipline is located just outside the information building and is operated by the corporation. The bus ride to the zipline starting point is about 30 minutes; the zipping is about 90 seconds.

The Bus Route to the Ziplines

4. **Walk in the Park:** A wide trail covered by beautiful huge evergreen trees in a serene park next to the information building is open for easy and free strolling. The trail loops in the park for about 3/4ter of a mile.

5. Walk/Shuttle to Hoonah: Hoonah is a fishing village about 2 miles from the cruise ship dock. A wide flat and beautiful sidewalk along the sea connects ISP to Hoonah. You can also, for a few dollars, take a shuttle to Hoonah.

Walk to Hoonah

6. Kayaking: ISP is surrounded by lands and mountains and the sea is normally calm and thus perfect for kayaking. Kayaking tours are offered by the ship or by the corporation at Hoonah.

7. Fish Packing Museum: located within a short walk from the information building and it is normally open for free.

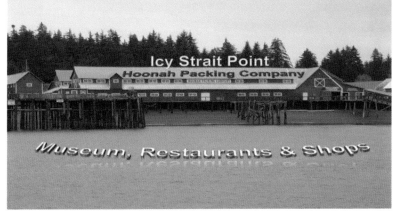

Icy Strait Point
Hoonah Packing Company

Museum, Restaurants & Shops

Restaurants: Several restaurants are on-site offer some of the best fresh seafood anywhere, King crab to salmon. Even though normally is pricing, it is worth the cost.

Shops: Several on-site shops, some with native and unique Tlingit products.

# Sitka, Alaska, USA

Location: on the west side of, the 100-mile-long, Baranof Island*. only accessible by air and sea; the 21 miles roadway along the Pacific coast does not bridge into other islands.

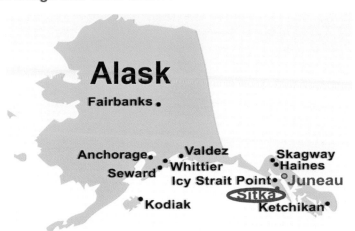

The Name Sitka: derived from *Sheet'ká*, a contraction of the native Tlingit *Shee At'iká* means "People on the Outside of **Baranof Island***," whose Tlingit name is *Sheet'-ká X'áat'l*.

*Baranof Island** was named after the first Russian governor of Russian America, Alexander Baranof.

Synopsis of History: the area was originally settled by the **Tlingit People**** over 10,000 years ago.

****The Tlingit:** Indigenous people of the Pacific Northwest Coast of North America.

Russian Explorers: settled Old Sitka in 1799, naming it Fort Saint Michael (Russian: форт Архангела Михаила). In June 1802, Tlingit warriors destroyed the original settlement, killing many of the Russians. The Russian came back in 1808 with large force and established the settlement "New Archangel", currently Sitka, which was designated the capital of Russian America.

Saint Michael Cathedral: In1848, the Russian built the Cathedral and became the seat of the Russian Orthodox bishop of Kamchatka, the Kurile and Aleutian Islands, and Alaska. Evidence of Russian settlement in names, Baranof & Chichagof Islands.

The Purchase of Alaska: The ceremony to transfer Alaska from Russia to the US was held in Sitka on October 18, 1867. Sitka remained the capital of Alaska after the purchase and until 1906 when it was transferred to Juneau due to the declining economic importance of Sitka.

World War II: The US Army and Navy built bases in the Sitka area to defend against Japan. These bases were deactivated by the end of the war.

Size: Sitka is the largest city, by area, in the USA (see US' Ten Largest Cities table in Juneau section in this book). The total area of Sitka is 4,811 miles^2 (12,460.4 km^2). This is almost four times the size of the state of Rhode Island.

Sitka Population: ~9,000 inhabitants.

8-Major Attractions: Most of these attractions are within walking distance from downtown Sitka. Shuttle buses normally operate between the port and downtown. Locations of these attractions are mapped in this section.

1. **Alaska Raptor Center:** a 17-acre raptor rehabilitation center to rehabilitate sick and injured eagles, hawks, falcons, owls, and other birds of prey that are brought in from all over Alaska. The Center is the largest of its type in Alaska. Located about 3 miles from downtown. The center is within walking distance from Sitka National Historical Park.

2. **Baranof Castle Hill:** also known as the **American Flag-Raising Site:** Located within walking distance from downtown Sitka. It is a National Historic Landmark and state park. It is the historical site of Russian and Tlingit forts. This is the location where Russian Alaska was formally handed over to the United States in 1867. Thus, this is where the 49-star US flag was first flown after Alaska became a state in 1959.

3. **Russian Bishop's House:** was the **Russian Mission Orphanage:** is a National Historic Landmark located at Lincoln and Monastery Streets. This log building was Completed in 1843. It is the oldest surviving buildings in Russian America. It was the home of the first Bishop of Alaska. The house is now an integral part of the National Park Service.

Russian Bishop's House

4. **St. Michael's Cathedral:** is an Orthodox cathedral located at Lincoln and Maksoutoft Streets. The original cathedral was built by Russia in the 19th century. This cathedral was burned down in 1966 and was subsequently rebuilt. It is a National Historic Landmark.

St. Michael Cathedral

5. **Sheldon Jackson Museum:** Native American museum founded in 1887, becoming the first museum in Alaska. The museum is owned by the State of Alaska. Over 5,000 artifacts housed in the museum. Located at College and Hillcrest Drives.

Sheldon Jackson Museum

6. **Sitka National Historical Park:** Was **Indian River Park:** The mission of the park is to commemorate the Tlingit and Russian experiences in Alaska. The park headquarters is about one mile from downtown Sitka.

7. **Fortress of the Bear:** is an educational **bear** rescue center located at 4639 Sawmill Creek Rd. Orphaned bears from the state of Alaska are brought here for rehabilitation and to find homes for them in zoos and sanctuaries internationally.

8. **Hiking:** Maps are available from the information center in downtown Sitka, where the shuttle bus route from the port terminates. Bear Pepper Spray is normally available from a vendor outside the information center. It is very advisable to carry a can of bear pepper spray with you if you are planning to hike in the forest.

Maps: The three successively enlarged Google Earth maps next page indicate the locations of the above major attractions. You need a shuttle bus to reach downtown Sitka from the cruise ship dock. You will need transportation to reach the Fortress of the Bear. All other attractions are within walking distance from downtown Sitka. The longest walk from downtown Sitka is to Alaska Raptor Center (about 2 miles through Sitka National Historical Park HQ). You can also use transportation to the Alaska Raptor Center.

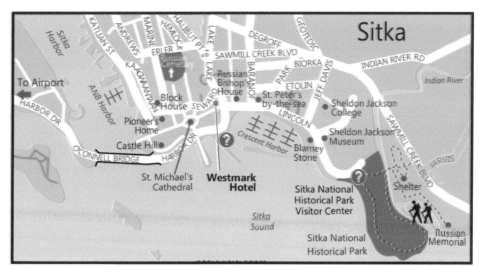

Map of Sitka

Climate data for Sitka											
Month	**Jan**	**Feb**	**Mar**	**Apr**	**May**	**Jun**	**Jul**	**Aug**	**Sep**	**Oct**	**Nov**	**Dec**
Rec. high °F (°C)	60 (16)	61 (16)	61 (16)	76 (24)	82 (28)	85 (29)	88 (31)	84 (29)	77 (25)	68 (20)	65 (18)	65 (18)
Ave. high °F (°C)	41 (5)	41 (5)	43 (6)	48 (9)	53 (12)	58 (14)	60 (16)	62 (17)	58 (14)	51 (10)	44 (7)	41 (5)
Ave. low °F (°C)	32 (0)	32 (0)	33 (1)	37 (3)	42 (6)	48 (9)	52 (11)	53 (11)	48 (9)	42 (5)	35 (2)	33 (1)
Rec. low °F (°C)	0 (−18)	−1 (−18)	4 (−16)	15 (−9)	29 (−2)	35 (2)	41 (5)	34 (1)	31 (−1)	20 (−7)	2 (−17)	1 (−17)
Ave. prec. In. (mm)	8.7 (222)	6.3 (159)	5.8 (148)	4.3 (108)	4.3 (108)	2.9 (73)	4.0 (101)	7.0 (178)	11.9 (301)	13.2 (334)	9.9 (250)	8.6 (218)

Endicott Arm & Dawes Glacier, Alaska, USA

Location: Located at the southern edge of **Ford's Terror Wilderness Area***. Endicott Arm is 30-mile long surrounded by granite cliffs, U-shaped valleys, waterfalls, drifting **icebergs**** and many wildlife. At its head is a spectacular **Tidewater Glacier*****. This 250-500 ft tall, 1000 ft thick midway and ½ mile wide is Dawes Glacier. The map at the end of this section indicates the location of Endicott Arm and Dawes Glacier

> ***Ford's Terror Wilderness Area:** in 1889 a naval crew member, named Ford, rowed a dinghy into the narrow entrance of the fjord at low tide. The tide came back through the narrow entrance trapping the dinghy in the icy turbulent currents for the next "terrifying" six hours.

> ****For iceberg classification see Hubbard Glacier section in this book.**

> ***** Tidewater Glacier:** Follows cycle of advance alternating with fast retreat over many years. Tidewater glacier is relatively insensitive to climate change.

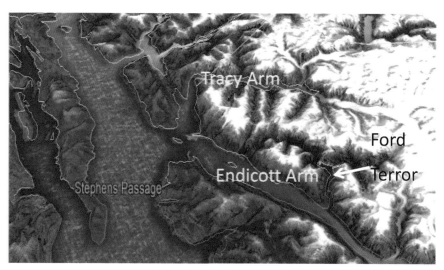

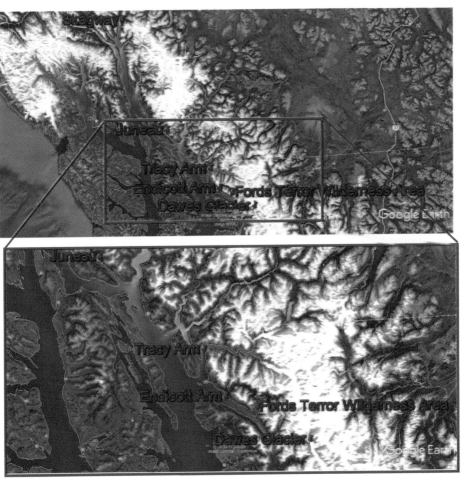

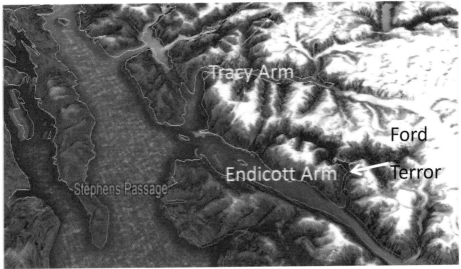

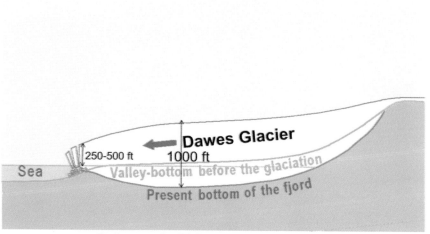

Schematic Side View of Dawes Glacier

Ford's Terror Wilderness Park (map at the end of this section): Area ~2643 km² (1020 ml²) contains 2 spectacular deep-water fjords with active tidewater glaciers at their termini: The fjords are Tracy Arm & Endicott Arm; the glaciers are Sawyer and Dawes. Both glaciers are ~30 mi (48 km) long. You will observe considerable floating ice in the two fjords during the summer months.

Endicott Arm Wildlife: A major breeding grounds for harbor seals. Other wildlife observed are brown bears, bald eagles, sea ducks, deer, moose, and wolves.

Harbor Seals Along Endicott Arm

Dawes Glacier

Sceneries Along Endicott Arm

Map of Ford Terror Wilderness Area

Ketchikan, Alaska, USA

Location: The south-easternmost city in Alaska is located on Revillagigedo Island. The Island was named in 1793 by Captain George Vancouver.

Synopsis of History: Ketchikan was founded in 1885 as a salmon cannery and thus, it was named "the Salmon Capital of the World". Later logging became an important industry and then on Aug 25, 1900, Ketchikan was incorporated as a city, the first incorporated city in Alaska. Therefore, adding these two firsts together, a new sign was erected on Mission Street **"Alaska's 1st City, the Salmon Capital of the World".**

Alaska's 1st City, the Salmon Capital of the World sign

Geography: Ketchikan is located 700 mi (1,100 km) north of Seattle, 235 mi (378 km) south of Juneau and surrounded by Tongass National Forest, the largest national forest in the US. The city covers an area of 5.9 mi^2 (15.3 km^2).

Population: about 8600; population density is 1,830/mi^2, Alaska's most densely populated city. The micropolitan population is about 14,000.

Topography: Deer Mountain, a 3,001 ft (915 m), rises immediately east of the city's downtown area.

Ketchikan and surrounding terrain (from the peak of Deer Mountain)

The Name Ketchikan: Named after Ketchikan Creek that originates from a lake. The creek is 6 miles (9.7 km) long and Empty into the **Tongass Narrows.** The historic **Creek Street** runs along the creek banks as a piling-perched boardwalk.

Ketchikan Creek Name: Comes from the native term "Katch Kanna "in the native Tlingit language that translates roughly into "spread wings of a thundering eagle". This imaginative name came from looking down at the area of Ketchikan from the top of Deer Mountain with little imagination.

Tongass Narrows: Y-shaped channel, part of the inside passage forms part of the Alaska Marine Highway. The ½ mile (800 m) wide channel separates Ketchikan from **Gravina Island** where Ketchikan airport is located.

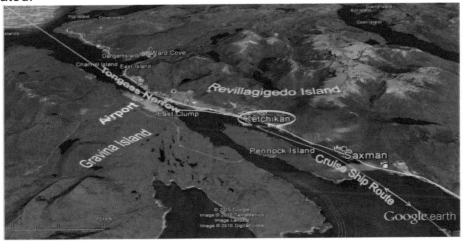

Gravina Island: named after Spanish Admiral Frederico Carlos Gravina by Spanish Explorer Jacinto Caamaño. Ketchikan airport is located on Gravina Island.

Bridge to Nowhere: was a proposed $398 million bridge to replace the ferry that currently connects Ketchikan with Gravina Island, where Ketchikan Airport and 50 residents live. The project encountered fierce opposition outside Alaska as a symbol of pork-barrel spending. The US Congress removed the federal earmark for the bridge in 2005 and canceled the project in 2015.

Ketchikan Airport is built on Gravina Island across Tongass Narrow from Ketchikan. Due to the scarcity of flat land, the airport is built on two levels. The lower level is where the tarmac and terminal building was built, and the higher level is where the runway is located. After loading passengers, a plane must climb one of two ramps to reach the runway. You can observe this uniquely built airport from the ship while the ship is approaching Ketchikan from the north or departing the city sailing northward.

Ketchikan Airport

5-Major Attractions: you can tour several during your ship's shortstop.

1. **Red-Light District:** early in the 20th century a red-light district formed near the mouth of Ketchikan Creek, Named **Creek Street***. Brothels were established on either side of the creek where both men & salmon came upstream to spawn.

Ketchikan Creek and Creek Street

   ***Creek Street: a** historic boardwalk perched on pilings along the banks of Ketchikan Creek. Today is a tourist attraction with Dolly's House museum and shop at locally-owned stores and galleries. During the Salmon Run, thousands of Salmon can be observed swimming upstream in the creek heading to their birth stream. The source of the creek is a lake 6 miles from the mouth of the creek at Creek Street.

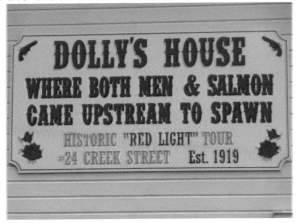

Spouses Quick Escape: during the heyday of the red-light district when the police raid the brothels, spouses looking for a quick exit to avoid a hefty fine & …. The **Married Man's Trail*** was the perfect escape route.

*Married Man's Trail: heads upward providing panoramic views of the town and harbor below.

Creek Street and Married Man's Trail are about 7 to 15 minutes' walk from the ship, depending on which berth was assigned to your ship.

Standing Totem Poles: Ketchikan claims that it has the world's largest collection of **Totem Poles***. You can find them throughout the city and at Saxman Totem Park**,** Totem Bight State Park**,** Potlatch Park**, and Totem Heritage Center**.

*The Totem** Poles: monumental symbols or figures sculptures carved on poles, posts, or pillars from large trees (i.e. western red cedar) by indigenous peoples of the Pacific

Northwest (NW) coast of North America (NW US & Canada's British Colombia).

> ****Totem Name and Symbol** derives from the Algonquian word odoodem "His kinship group ". May commemorate cultural beliefs, recount familiar legends, notable events, functional architectural features or/and welcome signs for village visitors.

2. **Totem Heritage Center:** the center is an interactive museum of old and new totem poles. You can reach the center through a short ride on the city bus from the port area. You can also stroll to the center along Creek Street and then Ketchikan Creek. The center is about 25 to 35 minutes' walk from your ship depending on the ship's berth location.

3. **Lumberjack Show:** will bring back childhood and sports fan competition memories. It is fun for the entire family. The show includes professional lumberjacks sawing stumps, rolling logs, and climbing poles in competition. Lumberjack Show is about 5 to 15 minutes' walk from your ship depending on where the ship is berthed.

4. **Hiking the 3,001 ft (915 m) Deer Mountain:** Trailhead starts at about 1.5 miles from the port. Take the city bus to Totem Heritage Center. The trailhead is about 15 minutes' walk from there.

Photo from Deer Mountain trail

5. **Misty Fjords National Monument:** a national monument & wilderness area. It is part of the Tongass National Forest. The monument is **about** 40 miles (64 km) from Ketchikan. You can take one of the ship tours to the monument or head to one of the **Information Centers** where private vendors sell tours to the monument.

Misty Fiords National Monument

Information Centers: Located just outside the ship's berths. They offer all you need to know regarding all attractions, including private tours, maps, directions, etc.…

Information Buildings

Ketchikan Port: The port can dock 4 large cruise ships. Walking distance to most attractions depends on which berth your ship is assigned to.

Location of Attractions

99950: Ketchikan's Zip Code: the highest in the country.

Climate data for Ketchikan												
Month	**Jan**	**Feb**	**Mar**	**Apr**	**May**	**Jun**	**Jul**	**Aug**	**Sep**	**Oct**	**Nov**	**Dec**
Rec. high °F (°C)	62 (17)	63 (17)	60 (16)	75 (24)	87 (31)	89 (32)	87 (31)	89 (32)	80 (27)	69 (21)	65 (18)	62 (17)
Ave. high °F (°C)	38 (3.6)	41 (5.2)	44 (6.4)	49 (9.6)	55 (12.8)	60 (15.8)	64 (17.8)	65 (18.1)	59 (15.1)	51 (10.4)	44 (6.4)	40 (4.4)
Ave. low °F (°C)	29 (−1.8)	31 (−0.4)	33 (0.6)	37 (2.6)	42 (5.4)	47 (8.4)	51 (10.8)	52 (11.2)	47 (8.4)	41 (4.8)	34 (1.2)	31 (−0.6)
Rec. low °F (°C)	−1 (−18)	0 (−18)	3 (−16)	10 (−12)	27 (−3)	33 (1)	39 (4)	37 (3)	29 (2)	17 (−8)	5 (−15)	−1 (18)
Ave. precip. In. (mm)	13.9 (353)	12.7 (324)	11.3 (287)	11.2 (284)	9.3 (235)	7.4 (187)	7.4 (189)	10.8 (274)	14.2 (361)	22.2 (563)	17.3 (438)	15.7 (398)
Ave. snow. in. (cm)	13.3 (33.8)	8.9 (22.6)	5.4 (13.7)	0.8 (2)	0.1 (0.3)	0 (0)	0 (0)	0 (0)	0 (0)	0.1 (0.3)	2.3 (5.8)	8.6 (21.8)

Dutch Harbor, Alaska, USA

Location: located on Unalaska and Amaknak Islands, part of the Fox Islands archipelago** of the Aleutian Islands groups*.

> ***Aleutian Islands Groups:** A chain of 14 large volcanic islands & 55 smaller ones, most belong to the US, except at the western end the small Commander Islands belong to Russia. The islands comprise five groups (east to west): The Fox Islands*, Islands of Four Mountains, Andreanof, Rat Islands, and Near Islands. The Aleutian Islands form part of the Aleutian Arc in the Northern Pacific Ocean. They are part of the Pacific Ocean Ring of Fire. Extending about 1,200 mi (1,900 km) westward toward Russia's Kamchatka.

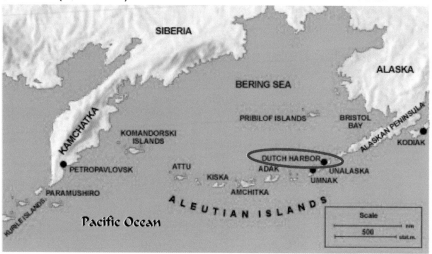

****Fox Islands:** The name was given by Russian explorers and fur traders. The Fox Islands comprise of (from west to east): Umnak, Unalaska***, Amaknak, Akutan, Akun, Unimak & Sanak.

*****Unalaska:** The largest of the Fox Islands archipelago. Unalaska city is the largest city in the Aleutian Islands.

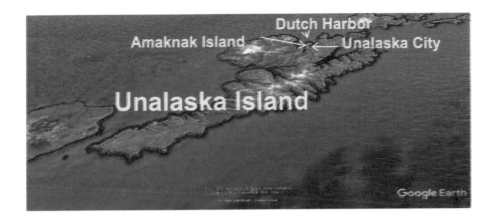

Unalaska City: Located on Unalaska & Amaknak Islands which are connected by a bridge called "the Bridge to the Other Side". Population ~4500, most are descendants of natives & Russians.

Unalaska City/Dutch Harbor

Name confusion: Unalaska is the name for both the island and the town. The harbor in front of the town is called Dutch Harbor and many literatures, shipping companies and the Federal Aviation Administration (FAA) refer to the Unalaska City as Dutch Harbor even though technically there is no town named Dutch Harbor on Unalaska Island.

Synopsis of History: The Aleut native people (Unagan) inhabited Unalaska for thousands of years. They developed a complex society and maritime culture in conjunction with hunting and fishing in the world's richest water for wildlife.

1759, the first Russian trader reached the island. By 1763, conflicts between the Russian fur traders and the Unalaska Natives (the Unagan) started to appear. The Unagan destroyed four Russian ships and killed 175 hunters/traders. The Russian regrouped and then conducted a massacre of many Natives. In 1774 Russia established a permanent trading post. The Russians exploited the native, demanded fur pelts. The natives accepted the Russian Orthodox Church after offering them support & children's education.

In 1788 the Spanish contacted the Russians in Alaska for the first time and they claimed Unalaska for Spain, calling it Puerto de Dona Marie Luisa Teresa.

In 1825, the **Russian Orthodox Church of the Holy Ascension** was built in Unalaska. Between 1836 and 1840, measles, chicken-pox and whooping-cough epidemics drastically reduced the population; by 1850 only 300 Aleuts lived in Unalaska.

The Russian Orthodox Church

On October 18, 1867, the United States purchased Alaska from Russia, making Unalaska part of the U.S. territory (see Alaska section in this book).

By 1895 Fur trade declined along with the sea otter population due to overhunting the otters. Non-Alaskan prospectors showed up looking to get rich from the Alaska gold rush.

Before World War II: In response to the Japanese war threat, two military installations built next to each other; these were the only military installations in the Aleutian Islands at that time.

World War II: June 3-4, 1942, the Japanese Navy attacked. 43 Americans & 1 Japanese died. By mid-1942, a submarine base was in place, with a squadron of U.S. Navy S-class submarines. The US military buildup peaked in 1943 at 10,151 sailors and 9,976 soldiers.

Post-World War II: 1947, the military installations were scrapped.

Growing Pain: Economic & population growth taxed the infrastructure to the limit. Unalaska was expanding to meet the needs of its citizens, employees, and travelers.

The Port: Dutch Harbor has become a year-round full-service deep-draft port providing all the fishing industry needs. Provides protection & repair for disabled or distressed vessels. Dutch Harbor is ice-free due to **Kuroshio Current***. It is close to some of the world's richest fishing seas. The port is featured in the Discovery Channel "Deadliest Catch".

> ***Kuroshio Current:** A north-flowing warm ocean current on the west side of the North Pacific Ocean. Part of the North Pacific Ocean gyre similar-to the Gulf stream in N. Atlantic Ocean.

Wildlife: The Bering Sea and the Aleutian Islands are home to 450 species of fish and invertebrates, 50 species of sea birds and 25 species of marine mammals.

Churches: Jesus Christ of Latter-day Saints; Russian Orthodox of the Holy Ascension of Christ; United Methodist; Unalaska Christian Fellowship; Saint Christopher-By-The-Sea Catholic Church.

Economy: Based primarily on commercial fishing, seafood processing, fleet services, and marine transportation. Dutch Harbor is ranked as a top fishing port with more than a billion dollars per year fishing economy. These include huge harvests of pollock & cod from the Bering Sea. The Bering

Sea has one of the world's largest continental shelf that supports a rich ecosystem.

Major Attractions: the location of the attractions is indicated on the Google map at the end of this section.

Aleutian World War II National Historic Area

Aleutian World War II National Historic Area

Museum of the Aleutians: The history and culture of the Aleutians and Unalaska. Opened in 1999.

Museum of the Aleutians

Church of the Holy Ascension: The current church was built in 1894, probably on the site of an 1826 church.

Church of the Holy Ascension

Location of Major Attractions

Climate data for Dutch Harbor, Unalaska

Month	Jan	Feb	Mar	Apr	May	Jun	Jul	Aug	Sep	Oct	Nov	Dec
Rec. high °F (°C)	58 (14)	54 (12)	61 (16)	58 (14)	60 (16)	73 (23)	75 (24)	81 (27)	74 (23)	65 (18)	57 (14)	59 (15)
Ave. high °F (°C)	36.8 (2.7)	37.3 (2.9)	38.6 (3.7)	40.9 (4.9)	46.1 (7.8)	51.7 (10.9)	56.8 (13.8)	58.9 (14.9)	54.0 (12.2)	47.3 (8.5)	42.6 (5.9)	39.0 (3.9)
Ave. low °F (°C)	28.1 (−2.2)	27.6 (−2.4)	28.3 (−2.1)	31.4 (−0.3)	36.7 (2.6)	41.9 (5.5)	46.0 (7.8)	47.7 (8.7)	43.5 (6.4)	37.2 (2.9)	32.1 (0.1)	30.3 (−0.9)
Rec. low °F (°C)	−8 (−22)	0 (−18)	2 (−17)	−5 (−21)	15 (−9)	30 (−1)	21 (−6)	30 (−1)	19 (−7)	2 (−17)	8 (−13)	5 (−15)
Ave. precip. In. (mm)	7.28 (185)	6.35 (161)	5.40 (137)	3.46 (88)	3.98 (101)	2.48 (63)	2.19 (56)	2.69 (68)	5.21 (132)	7.17 (182)	6.76 (172)	7.89 (200.)
Ave. snow in. (cm)	23.8 (60.5)	20.4 (51.8)	16.5 (41.9)	6.6 (16.8)	0.2 (0.5)	0 (0)	0 (0)	0 (0)	0 (0)	0.5 (1.3)	6.4 (16.3)	17.1 (43.4)

Vancouver, BC, Canada

Location: Southwest of the Province of British Colombia (BC) and southwest of Canada.

Ancient History: area inhabited at the end of the last ice age ~10,000 years ago. The vicinity shows archeological evidence of a seasonal encampment near the mouth of the Fraser River.

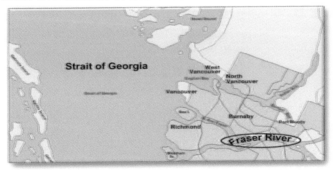

Modern History: 1791 Spanish Captain José María Narváez was the first European Explorer, a year later was followed by British **Captain George Vancouver***. However, the first European settler did not happen until 1862, 70 years after the first European explored the area.

> ***George Vancouver:** a British officer of the Royal Navy. In 1791–95 explored and charted North America's Northwest Pacific Coast and the Hawaiian Islands and the Southwest coast of Australia.

Vancouver Name (trivia): was given to several other geographical locations: in Canada, the city of Vancouver & Vancouver Island. In the USA, the city of Vancouver, Washington. In the USA & Canada border, Mount Vancouver on the Yukon/Alaska border (between Valerie & Hubbard Glaciers). In New Zealand, Mount Vancouver, the sixth highest mountain in the country.

Canadian Pacific Railway (CPR) Impact on Vancouver: 1880sThe CPR was extended to Vancouver. **Engine 374** pulled the first train into Vancouver in 1887. This engine is in a museum in the Yaletown community. The result of CPR operation was the rapid growth of the city due to Chinese railroad workers settled in the area followed by waves of immigration from Europe, Asia & other parts of the world.

Engine 374 in the Museum

Early Growth: 1863 Lumbering industry & 1st sawmill were operational. Their site is where Vancouver seaport today. 1886, the city was incorporated.

The Great Vancouver Fire of June 13, 1886: destroyed most of the city, dozens of lives were lost. Within 4 days, rebuilding started. By 1890, **Cordova Street** was back to normal operation.

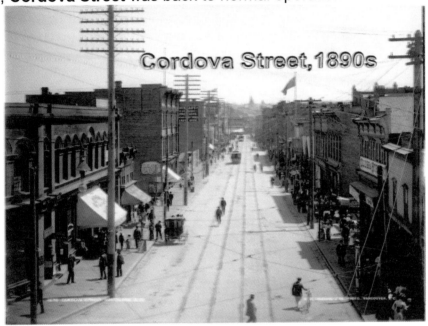

Port Development: 1923 Vancouver port was completed as one of the world's most technologically advanced port.

Depression Era: Vancouver managed to stave off bankruptcy. 1000s unemployed Canadians came to Vancouver looking for work. "Hobo jungles" sprouted up in several locations.

World War II: massive new spending by the governments coupled with military spending to upgrade the harbor defenses and military units to Europe to fight the war boosted the economy and terminated the depression.

1942 Japanese Canadian: after the Japanese attack on Pearl Harbor, Japanese Canadians were "evacuated" from the West Coast. Canadians of Japanese descent were placed interned in camps in the interior.

After World War II: extensive infrastructure developed/expanded: Bridges, airport, seaport, freeways; new corporations and institutes created. The film industries expanded and were called "Hollywood North". The results were a major increase in population.

Population: about 670,000 inhabitants, metro area is about 2.4 million inhabitants in the Greater Vancouver area. Vancouver is Canada's 3rd most populous metro area after Toronto and Montreal.

Population Density: city size is 114 km² (44 mi²) Land area. This equates to 5877 people/km² (15227 people/mi²), the most densely populated Canadian municipality; the 4th most densely populated city with over 250,000 residents in North America, after New York City, San Francisco, and Mexico City.

Languages: one of Canada's most diverse city; 52% of its residents have a first language other than English.

International City: Vancouver hosted many international conferences such as Commonwealth Games, UN-Habitat I, Expo 86, the World Police & Fire Games, the 2010 Winter Olympics, FIFA (Fédération Internationale de Football Association) games and others.

Ted's* Home: in 2014, after 30 years in California, the annual TED conference made Vancouver it's indefinite home.

*Ted (Technology, Entertainment, Design): a global set of conferences run under the slogan "Ideas Worth Spreading ". The early emphasis was technology & design consistent with its Silicon Valley origins. Currently, its focus broadened to include talks on many scientific, cultural & academic topics.

Geography: located on the Burrard Peninsula between Burrard Inlet to the north & the Fraser River to the south, the Strait of Georgia to the west. Shielded from the Pacific Ocean by Vancouver Island.

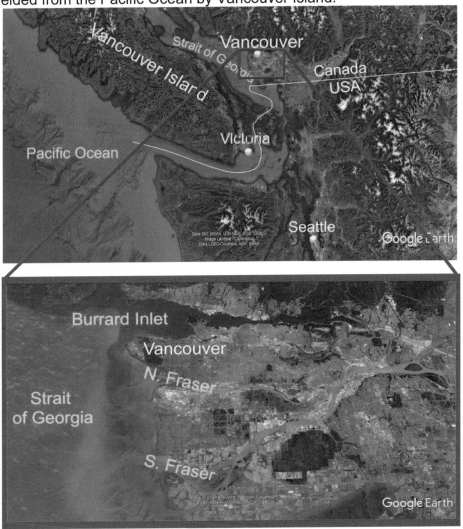

Japanese Flowering Cherry Trees: many streets are lined with these trees, flower for several weeks in early spring. They are celebrated by the Vancouver Cherry Blossom Festival normally held in April.

Japanese Flowering Cherry Trees

6-Major Attractions: this magnificent city deserves a few days at the beginning or the end of your cruise to discover its beauty and attractions.

1. **Canada Place:** this is the former Canada Pavilion from the 1986 World Exposition. It is the home of the Convention Center, the **Pan Pacific Hotel**, the main **cruise ships terminal**, and the World Trade Center. The exterior is covered by fabric roofs resembling sails.

Cruise Ship Port at Canada Place

2. **Pan Pacific Hotel:** part of Canada Place; cited as one of the best hotels in the city.

3. **Stanley Park:** is one of the largest urban parks in North America with an area of 405 hectares (1,001 acres). The park borders downtown Vancouver and is almost surrounded by water. Vancouver Aquarium is part of Stanley Park.

4. **Capilano Park:** Capilano Park is fun for the entire family: Its Suspension foot Bridge spans 137 m (450 ft) and towers 70 m (230 ft) above Capilano River is a breathtaking sight thrilling Since 1889. Includes seven Treetops bridges and challenging Cliff walk. The park is a private facility with admission tickets. 1.2 million

visitors per year. Normally, a free shuttle bus from Canada Place to Capilano park operates daily.

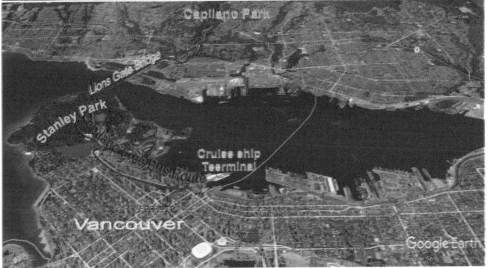

5. Granville Island: a hotspot for tourism, entertainment & shopping. Located under the south end of the Granville Street Bridge. The central location of several annual festivals. Granville Island includes Brewing Co with Beer tasting.

6. Science World: located at Telus World of Science, interactive exhibits and displays for the entire family.

Science World

Most Livable City: Vancouver ranked as one of the world's most livable cities and one of the world's cleanest cities. However, the city is also ranked among Canada's most expensive cities.

Cruise Ship Terminal to Airport: distance about 10 miles. You can take a taxi from Canada's Place for $26-$30 or walk about 650 meters to the metro, Waterfront Station, Canada Line and in 26 minutes for $2-$4 will take you to the airport.

Climate: Canada's second-warmest cities in winter and second-coolest city in summer after Victoria, the capital of British Colombia. The summer months are typically dry.

Climate data for Vancouver

Month	Jan	Feb	Mar	Apr	May	Jun	Jul	Aug	Sep	Oct	Nov	Dec
Rec. high °C (°F)	15.6 (60.1)	16.4 (61.5)	19.1 (66.4)	23.9 (75.0)	32.7 (90.9)	30.0 (86.0)	31.7 (89.1)	31.7 (89.1)	28.5 (83.3)	24.2 (75.6)	17.0 (62.6)	15.0 (59.0)
Ave. high °C (°F)	6.8 (44.2)	8.4 (47.1)	10.6 (51.1)	13.5 (56.3)	16.8 (62.2)	19.6 (67.3)	22.0 (71.6)	22.3 (72.1)	19.0 (66.2)	13.9 (57.0)	9.3 (48.7)	6.8 (44.2)
Ave. low °C (°F)	2.7 (36.9)	3.4 (38.1)	4.6 (40.3)	6.5 (43.7)	9.5 (49.1)	12.2 (54.0)	14.1 (57.4)	14.4 (57.9)	11.6 (52.9)	8.2 (46.8)	4.8 (40.6)	2.8 (37.0)
Rec. low °C (°F)	−13.3 (8.1)	−6.7 (19.9)	−5 (23)	−1.1 (30.0)	1.1 (34.0)	2.8 (37.0)	2.8 (37.0)	5.0 (41.0)	1.7 (35.1)	−3.2 (26.2)	−9.9 (14.2)	−15.6 (3.9)
Ave. precip. mm (inches)	178.8 (7.04)	183.8 (7.24)	155.8 (6.13)	117.9 (4.64)	86.7 (3.41)	69.9 (2.75)	53.4 (2.10)	50.8 (2.00)	73.3 (2.89)	147.8 (5.82)	239.2 (9.42)	231.3 (9.11)

 # Victoria, BC, Canada

Location: located on the southern tip of Vancouver Island.

Synopsis of History:

Before European Arrival: Coast Salish First Nations peoples established communities in the area for 1000s of years. The Coast Salish consists of several groups of ethnically related Indigenous peoples currently living in British Colombia, Washington, Oregon, southeast Alaska & Northern California.

Spanish and British Arrivals: part of the exploration of the northwest coast of North America by Spanish explorers Juan Pérez in 1774 and other Spanish sailors in 1790, 1791 and 1792 and British explorer James Cook in 1778.

Fort Victoria: 1841 the British (James Douglas) founded Fort Victoria on the site of present-day Victoria. 1843 the fort highlighted a permanent British settlement, Victoria. The impact of the fort was a negotiated settlement with the United States to Extend the British North America border with the USA along the 49th parallel from the Rockies to the Strait of Georgia. 1864 the fort was demolished and by 1924 the fort's site was designated a National Historic Site of Canada.

Model of Fort Victoria

The 49th Parallel Border with the USA

Location of Fort Victoria Site

The Gold Rush: 1858 gold was discovered on British Colombia (BC) mainland. Victoria became the supply base for miners increasing its population from 300 to 5,000. 1862 Victoria was incorporated as a city and in 1871 became the provincial capital when BC joined the Canadian Confederation.

Opium: 1870s large quantities of opium legally imported through Victoria's port from Hong Kong. 1908 the opium trade was banned negatively impacted Victoria's economy.

Railway to Vancouver Impact: 1886, Canadian Pacific Railway was extended to Vancouver. Victoria's position as the commercial center of BC was lost to Vancouver.

Victoria's natural setting enhanced by:

1. **Edwardian Baroque architectural buildings:** An architectural style popular during the reign of King Edward VII of the UK (1901 to 1910).

2. **Craigdarroch Castle built in the 1890s.**

3. **1904 opening of Butchart Gardens.**

4. **1908 construction of the Empress Hotel & later its Miniature World.**

5. Early in the 20th century opening the Hatley Park.

After World War II: the city experienced steady growth. Major universities and colleges initiated and expanded. Suburbs were incorporated and new infrastructures built and upgraded.

Historic Buildings: large number of historic buildings; the most famous are the Parliament Buildings (1897) and the Empress hotel (1908).

The Name and Uniqueness of Victoria: named after Queen Victoria of the UK (24 May 1819 – 22 Jan 1901); one of the oldest cities in the Pacific Northwest of North America; the southernmost city in Western Canada.

Population: approximately 88,000, metro population approximately 375,000; the 15th most populous Canadian metro area; the 7th most densely populated city in Canada at 4,400 people per Km^2, greater density than Toronto, Canada's largest city.

Economy: major components of the economy are technology, food products, tourism, and government: Federal & Province.

Geography: 100 km (60 mi) from Vancouver, BC; 100 km (60 mi) from Seattle, Washington, USA; 40 km (25 mi) from Port Angeles, Washington, USA. (see map).

Geographical Location of Victoria

Tourism: Victoria is a major tourist destination, 3.5 million overnight visitors per year, over 500,000 daytime visitors arrive via cruise ships & ferries. Tourism adds about one billion dollars to the local economy.

Major Attractions: Craigdarroch Castle, Butchart Garden, Empress Hotel, Hately Park, Beacon Hill Park, The Parliament, Crystal Garden, Royal British Colombia Museum, Maritime Museum, Chinatown, Art Gallery, Congregation Emanu-El synagogue, Church of our Lord, Victoria Conservatory of Music, and St. Andrews Cathedral.

Craigdarroch Castle: completed in 1890, built as a home for Robert and Joan Dunsmuir, the wealthiest people in British Columbia. The castle has an imposing exterior coupled with beautiful interior woodwork, stained glass, and Victorian artifacts.

Location of Craigdarroch Castle

Butchart Gardens was built in 1904 to beautify a quarry. The garden consists of 50 acres of botanical and other gardens, such as Rose, Japanese & Italian. Normally Bus tours from major hotels (~30 min. drive). Over one million visitors/year. Designated a National Historic Site of Canada.

Location of Butchart Garden

Empress Hotel: was built in 1908, by the Canadian Pacific Railways (CPR) Company. The hotel represents a type of architecture of CPR in Canada. Inside you will find unusual boutiques & displays featuring the history of the CPR. Tourists are welcomed.

Location of Empress Hotel

Hately Park and Hately Castle: completed in 1908. Consists of 565-acre gardens & forest of Douglas fir and western red cedar with trails. Hatley Castle is a Federal Heritage Building.

Location of Hatley Castle and Park

Beacon Hill Park: the park is central Victoria's main urban green space. 190   acres of game fields, gardens, exotic plants, and a petting zoo. From there you can view the Olympic Mountains in Washington state, USA.

The Parliament: located diagonally across from the Empress Hotel. The building is a Neo-baroque building on the inner harbor. A statue of Queen Victoria stands on the front; British Colombia's Cenotaph commemorating all Wars is on the front corner of the building. Free guided tours are offered year-round.

Location of Parliament

Crystal Garden: A glassed-roofed building located behind the Empress Hotel

Royal British Columbia Museum includes 3 galleries: The Natural History, the "First People's" (A history of BC native population) and Modern History.

Royal British Colombia Museum

Location of Royal BC Museum

Maritime Museum

Location of Maritime Museum

Chinatown: is the second oldest in North America after San Francisco's.

Chinatown

Location of Chinatown

Art Gallery of Greater Victoria

Location of Art Gallery of Greater Victoria

Congregation Emanu-El: the oldest synagogue on Vancouver Island and the oldest on the west coast of N. America. Was built in 1863 and is still in use. Declared as one of Canada's National Historic Site and one of BC's heritage properties.

Location of Congregation Emanu-El

- **Church of our Lord:** Historic Gothic church was built in 1870. Currently is a member of the Anglican Church in N. America. The church is a National Historic Site of Canada.

Location of Church of our Lord

Victoria Conservatory of Music

Location of Conservatory of Music

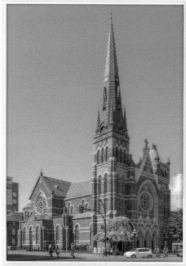

St. Andrew's Cathedral
Roman Catholic
Built in the High Victorian Gothic style

Location of St. Andrews Cathedral

Rogers Chocolates Store: located on Government Street near Broughton Street operational since 1885. They make the best chocolates in the world? You can also collect Christmas ornaments.

Location of Most Attractions: The most interesting sights are within walking distance of each other in downtown Victoria.

If you are pressed for time: walk around the inner harbor where the following sites are within easy walking distance from each other:

- **The Legislative Building (Parliament)**

- **The Empress Hotel**

- **The Royal British Colombia Museum**

- **Miniature World**

- **Maritime Museum**

- **Roger Chocolates Store**

Location of the Above Attractions

The Cruise Ship Port: normally a shuttle will operate between the port and downtown.

Climate: Normally, summer is dry & sunny. Winter is mild & rainy. Victoria is farther north than Ottawa, however, westerly winds & Pacific Ocean currents keep Victoria's winter temp higher than Ottawa (average. Jan. temp. 5.0 °C (41.0 °F) compared to Ottawa, −10.2 °C (13.6 °F)).

Climate Data for Victoria

	Jan	Feb	Mar	Apr	May	Jun	Jul	Aug	Sep	Oct	Nov	Dec
Avg. Tem °C	4.3	5.6	6.8	8.8	11.6	13.7	15.5	15.5	13.9	10.2	6.9	4.9
°F	40	42	44	48	53	57	60	60	57	50	44	41
Min. Temp °C	1.9	2.9	3.4	4.8	7.3	9.4	10.9	11	9.5	6.8	4.2	2.6
°F	35	37	38	41	45	49	52	52	49	44	40	37
Max. Temp °C	6.7	8.4	10.2	12.8	15.9	18.1	20.1	20.1	18.3	13.7	9.6	7.2
°F	44	47	50	55	61	65	68	68	65	57	49	45
Precip. mm	118	80	55	38	26	22	17	22	35	72	112	121
In	4.6	3.1	2.1	1.5	1.0	0.9	0.7	0.9	1.4	2.8	4.4	4.8

Printed in Great Britain
by Amazon

21807755R00062